'Mission is about finding out what God is doing and joining in.'

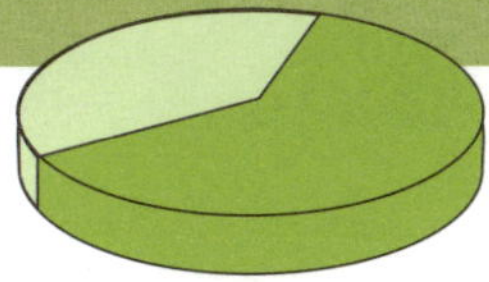

60% of the UK population find it difficult to connect with the Church

Before we begin . . .

As our culture changes, Christians are sowing the seed of the gospel into the lives of individuals and communities and beginning to grow fresh expressions of church. This has been happening for some time in circuits and parishes.

In 2004, the Church of England and the Methodist Church determined to encourage this movement. The Church of England published a best-selling report: *Mission-shaped Church: Church Planting and Fresh Expressions of Church in a Changing Culture.*

The Methodist Church refocused its priorities through a Conference Resolution. One of five areas of focus is 'encouraging fresh ways of being church'.

Both churches are now actively seeking to grow a 'mixed economy church':

- valuing and growing traditional churches
- starting fresh expressions
- connecting everything together so that the whole body grows

Watch the main programme on the Expressions DVD at this point as an introduction to fresh expressions of church

In *Moving on* we highlighted ten foundations for starting fresh expressions. They are all important. Four of them are about 'advance preparations' in the life of the Church so we haven't written more about them in this book but here is a reminder:

- build mission-centred values at the heart of the Church as it is
- pray
- prune a little so that church life is healthy and sustainable
- explore partnerships with others inside and beyond the churches

For more on values see Paul Bayes ***'Mission-Shaped Church – Missionary Values, Church Planting and Fresh Expressions of Church'*** **Grove Evangelism 67**

fresh expressions   The Methodist Church   THE CHURCH OF ENGLAND

For discussion

Do you have an understanding of the four elements discussed above?

Are you ready to move forward?

A mission-shaped process

The Church in Britain has been planting new churches for hundreds of years.

But most of those churches have been planted in a similar culture to that of the 'sending' church. If the culture was the same, it made sense to begin with a building, a minister and a service of worship. When the new church building opened its doors, a congregation gathered for worship. Over time, the congregation became a community and developed ways of making disciples and engaging in mission.

In our rapidly changing culture most people are no longer able to relate to church as it is. Fresh expressions of church therefore need to be shaped by mission. That means, in turn, a different process.

There are seven essential elements:

- **Prayer and support** given to the fresh expression by the wider church family.
- **Connections** between the fresh expression of church and the wider body of Christ. These connections will grow and change as you move forward.
- **Listening and following God's call** is the place where everything begins at each point in the journey. The listening is always twofold. We are listening to God on the one hand through the society in which we are called to work, and on the other hand through the Christian tradition. It is this 'double listening' which is at the heart of being mission-shaped.

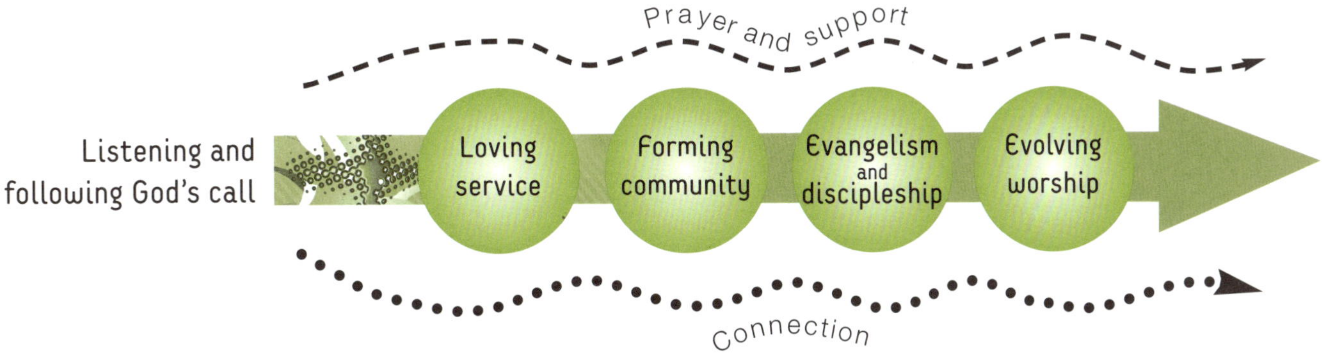

Different fresh expressions visit the other four circles in a different order. We've put them here in the order we think is most common.

- **Loving Service**
- **Forming Community**
- **Evangelism and Making Disciples**
- **Evolving Worship**

In mission to those furthest away from church life, most of the early investment of time and people will be in serving and forming community. Only as that creates a positive effect will it be realistic to expect evangelism and disciple making to take place. As people begin to meet Jesus, then it will make sense to explore how they worship.

Remember this process itself is only the beginning of a journey. There is much more to be said about how a fresh expression grows to maturity.

This map for the journey is based on our observation of many different stories all of which are different. Use it flexibly as a guide and starting point but not the final word. There is lots of learning still to do. Be ready to do some thinking in each of these areas.

For discussion

Do you recognize any of these elements in the map in your own experience or in stories you have researched? Which surprises you most? Which is the most important for your group at the moment?

Listening and following God's call

Listening to God and to the context is the starting point for letting mission shape the fresh expression. We need to grow big ears!

Focusing in

Mission-shaped Church chapter 1 helps us listen to the culture in which we do mission. The huge changes in society are so far reaching that it is more helpful to think that part of the Church's task is a cross-cultural mission.

Acts 17 tells us that when Paul went to Athens he spent his first days in the city listening and watching. We must do the same.

How to listen in neighbourhoods and networks

For neighbourhoods:

- stand on street corners
- read the local paper
- talk to others in a supermarket queue

Some Christians began community development work in Cardiff. Gill befriended Mary who invited her to the local school ground one night to show her the teenage drug abuse and promiscuity. 'When you tackle this I'll start believing', Mary said.

Conduct a mission audit to discover what the issues and needs are for local people. Look at the census results online for local wards.

The Eden projects noticed that there were many disaffected young people on deprived housing estates in Manchester; they work in youth clubs and schools and as detached youth workers to connect with these teenagers.

For networks:

- observe the patterns and places of physical meeting
- notice the methods and content of communication
- listen for the common issues

Find out who are the respected local opinion formers and networkers and ask them their views. Most communities have key people within them, sometimes called gatekeepers. Spend time with them to win their trust. They will open doors for you.

HOW MIGHT IT FEEL?

Overwhelming. What can we do?

Frustrating. Be patient; you have to enter a culture before you can effectively challenge it.

Uncomfortable as not all aspects of culture are good.

Surprising.

Inactive? Will listening be enough? No, but you must start there.

Very slow going. Take your time; the longer we sit with something the more we begin to see.

What are you listening for?

Listening with the first ear to the context – what is happening in wider society and in your locality (as explained on p. 4).

Listening with the other ear to the Christian tradition – how does the Christian faith speak to your particular situation? What can it bring to and how does it challenge what it meets?

Mission is finding out what God is doing and joining in.

So as you listen, ask God the questions: 'What are you doing? How do you want us to join in?'

The story of the healing at the pool in John 5 shows Jesus listening, watching, then acting. Even he needed that process. We follow his example but with a humility that acknowledges that, unlike Jesus, we do not have the ability to discern fully what God is doing.

Remember the more cross-cultural the context, the longer it will take you to understand what is really going on.

You may feel you aren't in control – but God is.

Discerning and testing a specific call from God

As you listen and ask and listen again, you will begin to discern God's call. This sometimes takes time (see Acts 16.6-10). Vision which comes from a God-given call is motivating and sustaining. Listen for such a call and test it out with trusted friends and then those to whom you are accountable. Be prepared to count the cost before you set out.

***'We must do something now!'* Yes, but listen and discern, then move to the next steps.**

Watch the story of *Somewhere Else* and *Legacy XS* for examples of how people listened and the vision formed and grew with them.

For discussion

Talk to one another about your experiences of listening to God. What do you believe God may be calling you to do? How can you discern if that call is genuine? Where do you sense God is already at work in your wider community?

Loving Service and Forming Community

These are related and happen in two ways. They are separated for clarity, but overlap in practice.

- The team serve people in the neighbourhood or network. This grows the sense of community.
- The team lives out being servants of one another, in the spirit of Christian community.

Notice the echoes in Mark 3.13-14: Jesus called the disciples, to be with him and to send them. Quality in relationships is the bedrock beneath sending and service.

Serving others

Mark 10.45 gives Jesus' summary of his purpose; to serve and lay down his life for others. Like Jesus, we go to where people are. He spent his ministry on the road, meeting people in their homes or at work. He didn't invite them to come to synagogue.

> *In developing a new youth congregation in Reading, the minister and his team did not start by putting on quality youth events. They went to the local schools offering trained support for excluded kids. As they won their trust, they could move on to events like film nights and discussion of how teenagers saw life.*

Service sows seeds of kindness. It undoes bad past impressions of the Church. It also helps people sense that they belong and enables community and friendship to grow.

Service which builds community does not seek to control. It avoids creating dependency. It is sustainable over the long term. It aims to empower people and to listen to them. It is able to receive as well as to give.

> *A small team in Coventry offers free hot drinks and a listening ear between midnight and 4 a.m. on the streets. After a year, the team have learned a great deal about serving others and discipleship. They are also seeing relationships and community grow but in unexpected ways.*

Through service, community grows naturally and is nurtured as people are able to spend time together in conversation. In the ministry of Jesus and today, meals are particularly important in developing these relationships.

> *Messy Church in Portsmouth provides after school craft activities for children and parents together with a meal and an act of worship.*

How might it feel?

Tempting to start with public worship but resist at this stage.

Lots of give for little gain.

Slow going.

'Can we dare to offer what we can?'

Challenging – to receive and not just to give.

Scary. Letting go of control can be frightening.

Learning to be a community of servants

Good teams are much more than a collection of talented individuals. Growing a community who will serve each other is vital. The leader sets the tone. Jesus showed this, in John 13, by washing the disciples' feet.

Depth of open honest relationships takes time and is demanding, because real lives are messy not neat. Real relationships are grown not imposed. They do grow through working and relaxing together.

So the two communities grow together as the serving unfolds through listening.

> *On an estate in Blackheath Christians discovered what local people wanted was their communal pond cleared. As a joint effort they all did it. A resident remarked, 'It used to be them and us and now we're in it together.'*

Vulnerability feels risky.

Acceptance is a delight.

'Is giving time to team selfish? **No, it's essential.**

Surprises are to be expected.

Breakthrough is beginning to happen.

Watch the stories of *Nightshift* and *Cable Street* to see how community has begun to grow up from a vision of listening and service.

For discussion

What gospel stories spring to mind when you think of loving service and forming community? How have you seen this at work already in different places? Are you called to work within existing communities and networks, or are you looking to create new communities?

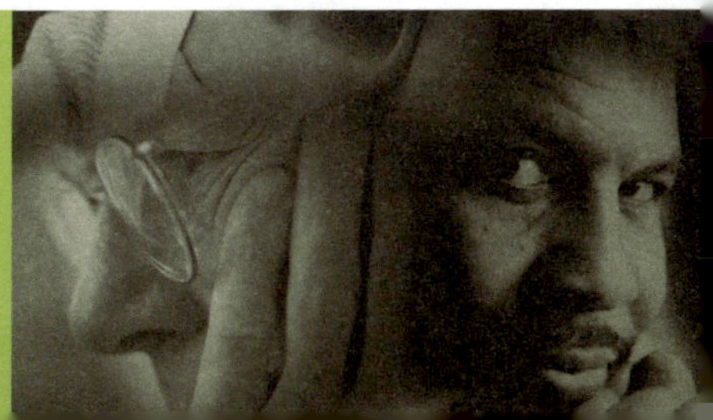

Evangelism and Making Disciples

Sometimes when you form community it can feel very natural then to share the Christian gospel. At other times you will need to think carefully about the right ways to share faith in a new context.

Again the foundation is **listening**:

- Listen to God for the right way forward.
- Listen to the people you are getting to know. What would be most helpful to them at this point?

There came a moment in the story of the meeting on the Emmaus road where Jesus changes from a listener to a teacher. Sensing the same moment in other people's journeys is vital.

Relationships and sharing lives

As we serve others and live out a quality of community among them it leads naturally to deeper relationships. Questions about life and what makes us tick tend to start.

All team members may need help towards a natural sharing of their faith story and discerning when this is appropriate. Some members of the team will be gifted evangelists and may need to be encouraged and equipped.

God is the best missionary and works ahead of us. We are his junior partners. Peter had to learn to be open to spiritual enquiry from a very unlikely source (Acts 10). Ask who is your equivalent to Cornelius?

Making the most of one-off events

In the context of shared lives, single events with some kind of Christian reflection can be a powerful way of helping people move towards faith. They can be low key and based around a supper and testimony or much bigger events.

> *One church in Boldmere holds a regular pub night on life issues called 'Pints of View'. Another church in a large village in Buckinghamshire hosts a café church morning on the first Sunday of the month with a 20-minute presentation on a life issue at the heart of each event.*

How might it feel?

You need to keep listening to be open.

Sowing takes time but stay patient.

'Are enthusiasts safe?' **No, but you need them.**

Surprising, humbling and risky.

Responsive. Let the mission shape what sort of church is needed.

Learning the faith

Many people who grow towards faith may need an extended time of learning normally in the context of a group or community. This may be inside or outside the main setting of the group you are working with.

Unshockable grace is better than control.

You may find you can use one of the established courses but you may need to design something around your own group which starts further back.

Jesus calls people to full commitment and whole life discipleship. People need care and nurture for the first years of their Christian lives in order to become established as Christians. The learning continues all our lives.

> *In Merthyr Tydfil a group of 30 people came to the end of an Alpha course, had encountered Jesus – but didn't want to transfer to parish communion services. So they started a new congregation run in Alpha style.*

Listen to what life style issues emerge for new Christians. Help them bring together following Jesus and being in the real world. Expect that behaviour changes last, after belonging and believing are in place.

Watch the stories of *Mind the Gap* and *Taste and See* for examples of how individuals have come to faith and are growing in faith through fresh expressions.

For discussion

How can your core group best learn about sharing faith with others in natural and unforced ways? How do you imagine that someone will encounter the Christian gospel in the fresh expression of church which you are beginning?

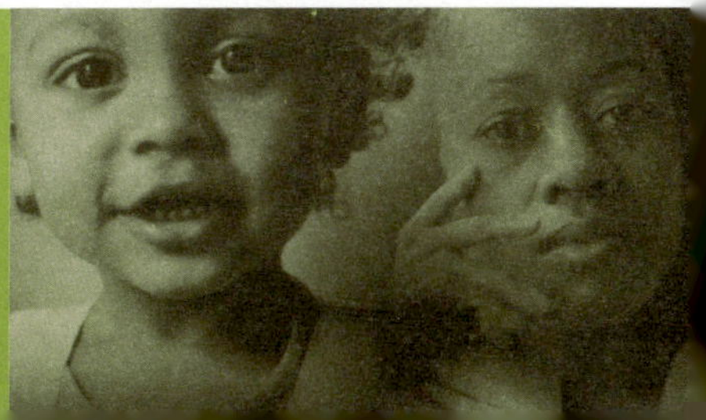

Evolving Worship

Worship is response to God's grace. We worship because of who God is and because of God's love revealed in Christ. Worship also grows out of the particular life of the faith community. This explains why worship at the end of something like a church weekend away often has a special quality.

How might it feel?

Aim to evolve worship that nurtures the community's life. It should connect with its calling and identity as a fresh expression of church.

Continual discovery.

How we understand the essence of worship is changing. For Anglicans, the emphasis used to be on authorized texts. Now there are agreed shapes to our services with options of texts to use at various points. The authors think change may go further and become based on values beneath the varying shapes.

Responsive not predetermined.

Worship does not evolve spontaneously. Those responsible for ministry within the fresh expression need first to listen, then to exercise their imagination: how can we best help this community to offer praise and prayer and engage with Scripture and sacraments? Getting there may be a process of trial and error and more listening.

No longer doing meals on wheels [provided centrally, just heat up] but learning to cook.

Mission shapes the starting point for church. An after school service will take a school assembly as a starting point because this is familiar territory. A lunch club for older people may offer a Prayer Book Eucharist for the same reason.

> *In Sheffield, Christians in mission to the work place met to worship in a room in Pizza Hut. They included sharing stories of what God was doing and response to God in prayer.*
>
> *An Anglo-Catholic parish in Yorkshire listened to young mums who didn't come on a Sunday, found out what they wanted and started all-age Monday Communion after school.*

As churches we place particular importance on the sacraments of Holy Communion and Baptism. Some fresh expressions have these as part of their worship and life from an early stage. Some take time to grow a sacramental life as they grow to become a mature church.

Making patterns that reinforce lessons learnt.

> *A priest in the North West listened to his wife. She told him Asda was where most people from the community were gathered. With permission he started Mass in the entrance concourse before the store opened for business.*

For all fresh expressions of church there is a sense of journey and of learning about worship together.

Prayer will focus on celebrating the story God is unfolding locally, living out the values of the fresh expression and fulfilling the mission calling.

Find what fits from the past and discover the songwriters, poets, artists in your own community. Grow your own material and borrow what fits.

> *Northumbria Community liturgies are written to help its members pray together through three questions that characterized the community's search. Who is it that you seek? How then shall we live? How shall we sing the Lord's song in a foreign land?*

Drawing on lessons from now and the past.

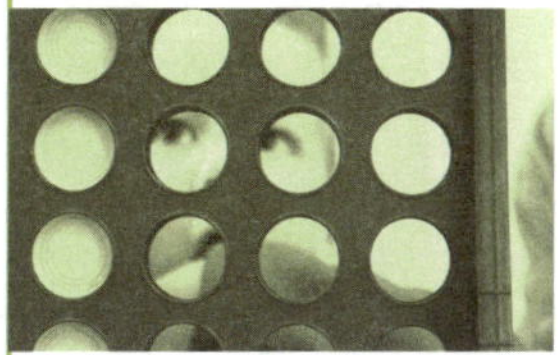

Watch the stories of *Sanctuary* and *Messy Church* for examples of the way worship is developing in two very different fresh expressions.

For discussion

Make a list of all the things your own group values about worship. Think of a group outside the church community with a very different culture (perhaps the group or network where you may be thinking of starting a fresh expression). Cross everything off the list which that group would find difficult in worship. Where should you begin in evolving worship that will be helpful?

Connection throughout the journey

Both Methodists and Anglicans know that the Church is more than just local. We call it being catholic. It reminds us of the Church being universal. It focuses our identity as essentially connected to the rest of Christ's people. It teaches us we are only a little part of the whole and we need others. It keeps us humble and gives us support.

Diversity without connection is a recipe for division and making sects.

Connection without diversity is a recipe for sterility and hinders renewal.

Connection is both organic and structural. Both are needed.

Organic connection is about strengthening relationships between people in a fresh expression and local traditional churches (or other fresh expressions).

> *A large suburban church has a separate and thriving youth congregation. The different congregations find it hard to worship together – no one is satisified. However, they really enjoy eating together and have a number of barbecues and social events during the year which build organic connection.*

Structural connection is also important. How is the fresh expression connected to the circuit, parish, deanery, district or diocese? How is it recognized as a legal entity? How will these relationships change as it grows to maturity? How can the two learn from each other?

There are lots of good examples and models around the country now. The Church of England is changing its legal structures to help this process forward through the new Dioceses, Mission and Pastoral Measure (more details on the fresh expressions web site).

Paul spoke of the church as the body of Christ and taught that we are all parts, like it or not. These aspects of a deep yet wider belonging must not be forgotten by pioneers as they blaze trails.

Those called to start something and those who give an enabling blessing from the wider Church need each other. It is together that they best bring to birth something creative and accountable. It helps get a good start and gives a framework that will sustain.

What does it feel like?

Supportive. Know you need others and they need you to give to them.

Growing in humility and valuing interdependence.

A maturing process – getting on with those not like us and who have different roles.

Watch the story of *Sanctus* for the importance of connection and the way this works out in practice.

For discussion

How will you take care to maintain and build these connections in the life of your fresh expression at the very beginning? How do you imagine these connections will need to change and grow as you move forward?

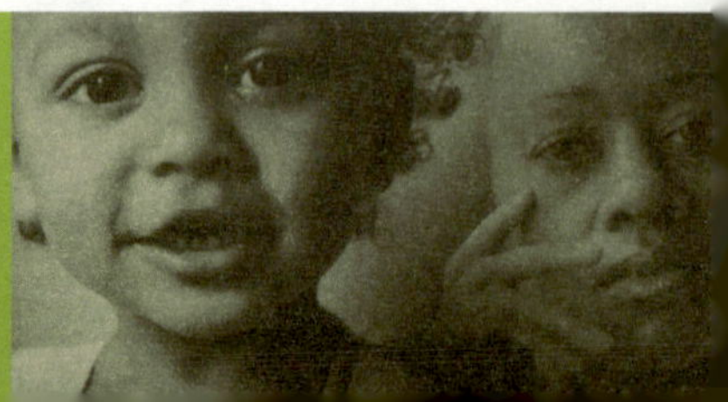